Table of Content

Sweet Stripes, *page 7*

Bambini, *page 22*

Seeds & Cables Topper, *page 9*

Baby, You're a Star!, *page 14*

True Baby Blue, *page 16*

Happy Elephants

This beanie will warm both your heart and those of passersby with its adorable elephant design. This is a great project for practicing your chart-reading skills too.

Design by Lena Skvagerson for Annie's Signature Designs

Skill Level

■■■□ INTERMEDIATE

Sizes

3–18 (18–24) months

Instructions are given for smaller size, with larger size in parentheses. When only 1 number is given, it applies to both sizes.

Finished Measurements

Circumference: 14 (16) inches

Height: 7½ (8½) inches

Materials

- Cascade Yarns Cherub DK (DK weight; 55% nylon/45% acrylic; 180 yds/ 50g per skein): 1 skein each turquoise #12 (A) and chocolate #24 (B)
- Size 4 (3.5mm) 16-inch circular and double-point needles (set of 5) or size needed to obtain gauge
- Stitch markers
- Cardboard

Gauge

24 sts and 32 rnds = 4 inches/10cm in St st.

To save time, take time to check gauge.

Special Abbreviation

Slip marker (sm): Slip marker from LH to RH needle.

Pattern Note

When working the chart and stranding colors, carry yarn loosely on the wrong side of fabric to prevent bunching.

Beanie

With A, cast on 84 (96) sts on double-point needles (smaller size) or circular needle (larger size), pm for beg of rnd and join, being careful not to twist.

Work in St st until piece measures 2¼ (2¾) inches.

Change to circular needle in smaller size.

Join B and work all rnds of Elephant Chart.

When chart is complete, piece should measure approx 5¼ (6½) inches in length.

Shape Crown

Note: *Change to dpns when sts no longer fit comfortably on circular needle.*

Cut B and continue with A.

Next rnd: *K14 (16), pm; rep from * around—6 markers.

Rnd 1: K2tog, *knit to 2 sts before marker, ssk, sm, k2tog; rep from * around until 2 sts rem, ssk—72 (84) sts.

Rnd 2: Knit.

Rep [Rnds 1 and 2] 5 (6) times—12 sts.

K2tog around—6 sts.

Cut yarn, leaving a 12-inch tail.

Use tapestry needle to run tail through rem sts twice, pulling securely and then fastening off.

Finishing
Weave in ends.

Tassel
Cut 2 pieces of B each 10 inches long. Cut piece of cardboard 2 inches long. Wrap B around cardboard 16 times. Cut yarn. Use tapestry needle to pull a 10-inch strand under all wraps at top of cardboard, then tie a knot to bundle the wraps. Cut yarn wraps at bottom of cardboard. Wrap 2nd 10-inch strand around bundle approx ½ inch below fold to form tassel. Trim ends.

Cut a 35-inch strand of B. Fold in half and secure folded end to a stationary object. Twist yarn until it begins to double back on itself. Pull end through fold on tassel. Fold in half again with both ends tog and allow to twist up on itself. Thread cord through top of hat and tie ends tog in a knot. Trim ends close to knot. ●

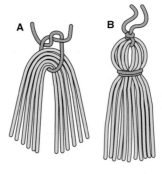

Tassel

STITCH KEY	
▨	A
■	B

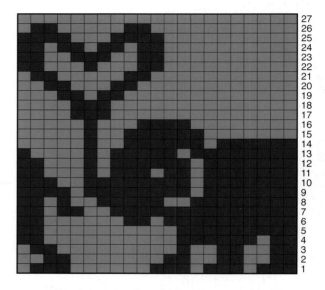

ELEPHANT CHART (SIZE 3–18 MONTHS)

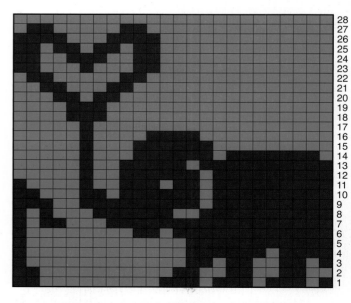

ELEPHANT CHART (SIZE 18–24 MONTHS)

Cherise

Subtle decreases are used to knit this beanie. Play around
with color for a fun look, then foray into appliqués
with this precious mini-heart for added flair.

Design by Trine Lise Høyseth

Skill Level

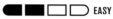 EASY

Sizes

0–3 (3–18, 18–24) months

Instructions are given for smallest size, with larger
sizes in parentheses. When only 1 number is given,
it applies to all sizes.

Finished Measurements

Circumference: 14 (16, 18) inches

Height: 6 (7, 8) inches

Materials

- Berroco Comfort (worsted
  weight; 50% nylon/50% acrylic;
  210 yds/100g per skein): 1
  skein each raspberry coulis
  #9717 (A) and
  pot-au-feu #9834 (B)
- Size 8 (5mm) needles or size needed
  to obtain gauge
- Size 7 (4.5mm) crochet hook
- Small stitch holder

Gauge

18 sts and 36 rows = 4 inches/10cm in garter st.

To save time, take time to check gauge.

Beanie

With A, cast on 27 (32, 36) sts.

Row 1 (WS): Knit.

Change to B.

Rows 2 and 3: K23 (28, 32) sts; turn, knit back.

Rows 4 and 5: K16 (20, 23) sts; turn, knit back.

Change to A.

Row 6 and 7: Knit.

Rep Rows 2–7 until work measures approx 12 (14, 16) inches along widest edge, ending with Row 7.

Bind off with A.

Cut yarn. Sew tail through sts on top and tighten.

Sew cast-on edge and bind-off edge tog, forming back seam.

Edge

With A, work rev sc (see page 29) along lower edge of beanie.

Heart Appliqué

With A, cast on 3 sts.

Row 1 (RS): Knit

Row 2: K1, yo, k1, yo, k1—5 sts.

Rows 3, 5, 7, 9 and 11: Knit, making sure to knit all yo's tbl.

Row 4: K1, yo, k3, yo, k1—7 sts.

Row 6: K1, yo, k5, yo, k1—9 sts.

Row 8: K1, yo, k7, yo, k1—11 sts.

Row 10: K1, yo, k9, yo, k1—13 sts.

Rows 12–16: Knit.

Row 17: K7; place rem 6 sts on holder.

Row 18: Knit.

Row 19: K2tog, k3, k2tog—5 sts.

Row 20: Knit.

Row 21: K2tog, k1, k2tog—3 sts.

Cut yarn, leaving an 8-inch tail.

Use tapestry needle to run tail through rem sts, pulling securely and then fastening off.

Rejoin A on Row 17 and with RS facing, pick up and knit 1 st (at center point of heart), k6 from holder.

Work Rows 19–21 as before.

Cut yarn, leaving an 8-inch tail.

Use tapestry needle to run tail through rem sts, pulling securely and then fastening off.

Finishing

Sew heart on side of beanie.

Weave in ends. ●

Sweet Stripes

This otherwise classic hat gets a fresh update with modern colors and a beautiful starburst at the crown.

Design by Lena Skvagerson
for Annie's Signature Designs

Skill Level

◕◼◻▭ EASY

Sizes

0–3 (3–18, 18–24) months

Instructions are given for smallest size, with larger sizes in parentheses. When only 1 number is given, it applies to all sizes.

Finished Measurements

Circumference: 11¾ (14½, 16) inches

Height: 7 (8, 9) inches

Materials

- Sirdar Snuggly DK (DK weight; 55% nylon/45% acrylic; 179 yds/ 50g per skein): 1 skein purple #197 (A)
- Plymouth Yarn Dreambaby DK (DK weight; 50% microfiber acrylic/50% nylon; 183 yds/ 50g per skein): 1 skein lilac #0107 (B)
- Size 6 (4mm) 16-inch circular and double-point (set of 5) needles or size needed to obtain gauge
- Stitch markers

Gauge

22 sts and 30 rnds = 4 inches/10cm in St st.

To save time, take time to check gauge.

Pattern Notes

When working in stripes, carry yarn not in use on wrong side of hat.

When stranding the colors at the crown, carry yarn loosely on the wrong side of fabric to prevent bunching.

Hat

Using double-point needles for the smallest size and circular needle for the larger sizes, with A, cast on 64 (80, 88) sts; pm for beg of rnd and join, being careful not to twist.

Work in St st until piece measures 2¼ (2¼, 2½) inches.

Rnds 1 and 2: Work in St st with B.

Rnds 3 and 4: Work in St st with A.

Rep [Rnds 1–4] 3 (4, 5) more times.

Drop B and continue working in St st with A only until piece measures 4¾ (5¾, 6¾) inches.

Continuing with both colors, work as follows:

Rnd 1: *K1 B, k7 A; rep from * around.

Rnd 2: *K2 B, k5 A, k1 B; rep from * around.

Rnd 3: *K3 B, k3 A, k2 B; rep from * around.

Rnd 4: *K4 B, k1 A, k3 B; rep from * around.

Tip

When working in stripes, carry yarn not in use on the inside.

Shape Crown

Note: *Change to dpns when sts no longer fit comfortably on circular needle.*

Cut A and continue with B only.

Set-up rnd: *Pm, k8; rep from * around—8 (10, 11) markers.

Rnd 1: *Slip marker, k2tog, knit to next marker; rep from * around—56 (70, 77) sts.

Rnd 2: Knit.

Rep [Rnds 1 and 2] 5 times—16 (20, 22) sts.

Next rnd: K2tog around—8 (10, 11) sts.

Cut yarn, leaving a 12-inch tail.

Use tapestry needle to run tail through rem sts twice, pulling securely and then fastening off.

Finishing
Weave in ends. ●

Seeds & Cables Topper

Hone your cabling skills with this earflap beanie. Then add visual interest and dimension with seed stitch.

Design by Lena Skvagerson for Annie's Signature Designs

Skill Level

■ ■ ■ ▢ INTERMEDIATE

Sizes

3–18 (18–24) months

Instructions are given for smaller size, with larger size in parentheses. When only 1 number is given, it applies to both sizes.

Finished Measurements

Circumference: 14 (16) inches

Height: 7 (8) inches

Materials

- Cascade Yarns Cherub Aran (worsted weight; 55% nylon/45% acrylic; 240 yds/100g per skein): 1 skein blue mirage #41
- Size 8 (5mm) 16-inch circular and double-point needles (set of 5) or size needed to obtain gauge
- Stitch marker
- Stitch holders
- 2 (¾-inch) buttons

Gauge

17 sts and 28 rnds = 4 inches/10cm in Seed St.

To save time, take time to check gauge.

Special Abbreviations

Make 1 Left (M1L): Insert tip of LH needle from front to back under strand between sts; knit into the back of the loop.

Make 1 Right (M1R): Insert tip of LH needle from back to front under strand between sts; knit into the front of the loop.

2 over 2 Right Cross (2/2 RC): Slip next 2 sts to cn and hold in back, k2, k2 from cn.

2 over 2 Left Cross (2/2 LC): Slip next 2 sts to cn and hold in front, k2, k2 from cn.

Pattern Stitches
Seed St

Rnd 1: *P1, k1; rep from * around.

Rnd 2: *K1, p1; rep from * around.

Rep [Rnds 1 and 2] for pat.

Cable (multiple of 10 sts)

Note: A chart is provided for those preferring to work pat st from a chart.

Rnd 1: *P4, k6; rep from * around.

Rnd 2: *P4, k2, 2/2 RC; rep from * around.

Rnd 3: Rep Rnd 1.

Rnd 4: *P4, 2/2 LC, k2; rep from * around.

Rep [Rnds 1–4] for pat.

Strap
Using circular needle, cast on 4 sts.

Row 1 (RS): Sl 1 pwise, p1, k2.

Row 2: Sl 1 pwise, k1, p1, k1.

Rep [Rows 1 and 2] until strap measures approx 12 (14) inches, ending with a RS row.

Earflap

Row 1 (WS): Sl 1 pwise, M1L, k1, p1, M1R, k1—6 sts.

Row 2: Sl 1 pwise, *k1, p1; rep from * until 1 st rem, k1.

Row 3: Sl 1 pwise, M1L, *p1, k1; rep from * until 1 st rem, M1R, k1—8 sts.

Row 4: Sl 1 pwise, *p1, k1; rep from * until 1 st rem, k1.

Row 5: Sl 1 pwise, M1L, *k1, p1; rep from * until 1 st rem, M1R, k1—10 sts.

Rep [Rows 2–5] 2 (3) times—18 (22) sts.

Next row (RS): Rep Row 2.

Next row: Work same as Row 4. Place rem sts on a holder.

Make another strap and earflap piece, and place on a holder.

Front Flap
With circular needles, loosely cast on 18 (20) sts.

Knit 2 rows.

Row 1 (WS): Sl 1 pwise, *k1, p1; rep from * until 1 st rem, k1.

Row 2: Sl 1 pwise, *p1, k1; rep from * until 1 st rem, k1.

Rep [Rows 1 and 2] until flap measures 2½ (2¾) inches, ending with a RS row. Place front flap on a holder.

Hat
Rnd 1: Using cable cast-on (see page 29), cast on 3 sts; continuing in Seed St as established, work across RS of first earflap, work across WS of front flap, work across RS of 2nd earflap, cable cast-on 3 sts—60 (70) sts.

Pm for beg of rnd and join, being careful not to twist.

Rnds 2–9: Work in Seed St.

Rnd 10: *M1L, k6 (7); rep from * around—70 (80) sts.

Remove marker, k3 (8), replace marker to indicate new beg of rnd.

Work Cable pat until piece measures 5 (6)inches, measured from Rnd 1 of hat, ending with Rnd 4 in pat.

Shape Crown

Note: *Change to dpns when sts no longer fit comfortably on circular needle.*

Rnd 1: *P2tog, p2, k6; rep from * around—63 (72) sts.

Rnd 2: *P3, k2, 2/2 RC; rep from * around.

Rnd 3: *P1, p2tog, k6; rep from * around—56 (64) sts.

Rnd 4: *P2, 2/2 LC, k2; rep from * around.

Rnd 5: *P2tog, k6; rep from * around—49 (56) sts.

Rnd 6: *P1, k2, 2/2 RC; rep from * around.

Rnd 7: *P1, k4, k2tog; rep from * around—42 (48) sts.

Rnd 8: *P1, 2/2 LC, k1; rep from * around.

Rnd 9: *P1, k2tog, k3; rep from * around—35 (40) sts.

Rnd 10: *P1, 2/2 RC; rep from * around.

Rnd 11: *P1, [k2tog] twice; rep from * around—21 (24) sts.

Rnd 12: *P1, k2; rep from * around.

Rnd 13: *P1, k2tog; rep from * around—14 (16) sts.

Rnd 14: K2tog around—7 (8) sts.

Cut yarn, leaving a 12-inch tail.

Use tapestry needles to run tail through rem sts twice, pulling securely and then fastening off.

Weave in ends.

Finishing

Fold up front flap and tack to hat across top. Sew a button through both layers in each upper corner. ●

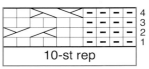

10-st rep

CABLE CHART

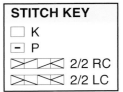

STITCH KEY

☐ K

– P

2/2 RC

2/2 LC

Gnome Whimsy

The perfect project to work on your decreasing skills, this beanie adds a whimsical twist to any child's wardrobe.

Design by Trine Lise Høyseth

Skill Level

 EASY

Sizes

0–3 (3–18) months

Instructions are given for smaller size, with larger size in parentheses. When only 1 number is given, it applies to both sizes.

Finished Measurements

Circumference: 14 (16) inches

Height: 12 (14) inches

Materials

- Berroco Comfort DK (DK weight; 50% nylon/50% acrylic; 178 yds/ 50g per skein): 1 skein each barley #2703 (A) and hummus #2720 (B)
- Size 3 (3.25mm) double-point (set of 5) needles
- Size 5 (3.75mm) double-point (set of 5) needles or size needed to obtain gauge
- Stitch markers

Gauge

24 sts and 32 rnds = 4 inches/10cm in St st.

To save time, take time to check gauge.

Beanie

With smaller dpns and A, cast on 72 (84) sts; pm for beg of rnd and join, being careful not to twist.

Rnd 1: Purl.

Drop A and join B.

Rnd 2: Knit.

Rnds 3–7: *K2, p2; rep from * around.

Rnd 8: With A, knit.

Rnd 9: Purl.

Rnd 10: With B, knit.

Rnd 11: Purl.

Change to larger needles.

Rnds 12–15: With A, knit.

Rnd 16: With B, knit.

Rnd 17: Purl.

Rep [Rnds 12–17] until work measures approx 4 (5) inches.

Shape Top

Rnd 1: With A, knit.

Rnd 2: *K4 (5), k2tog; rep from * around—60 (72) sts.

Rnds 3 and 4: With A, knit.

Rnd 5: With B, knit.

Rnd 6: Purl.

Rnd 7: Rep Rnd 1.

Rnd 8: *K8 (10), k2tog, pm; rep from * around—54 (66) sts.

Rnds 9–12: Rep Rnds 3–6.

Rnd 13: Rep Rnd 1.

Rnd 14: *Knit to 2 sts before next marker, k2tog, sm; rep from * around—48 (60) sts.

Rnds 15–18: Rep Rnds 3–6.

Rep [Rnds 13–18] 4 (6) more times—24 sts.

Remove markers.

Tail

Rnd 1: With A, knit.

Rnd 2: *K6, k2tog, pm; rep from * around—21 sts.

Rnds 3 and 4: With A, knit.

Rnd 5: With B, knit.

Rnd 6: Purl.

Rnd 7: Rep Rnd 1.

Rnd 8: *Knit to 2 sts before next marker, k2tog, sm; rep from * around—18 sts.

Rnds 9–12: Rep Rnds 3–6.

Rep [Rnds 7–12] 4 more times—6 sts.

With A, knit 3 rnds.

Cut yarn, leaving an 8-inch tail.

Use tapestry needle to run tail through rem sts, pulling securely and then fastening off.

Finishing

Weave in ends. ●

AnniesCraftStore.com   13

Baby, You're a Star!

With its unique shape and eye-catching pompoms, this beanie is sure to get your little one the attention any star deserves.

Design by Trine Lise Høyseth

Skill Level

■■□□ EASY

Sizes

0–3 (3–18, 18–24) months

Instructions are given for smallest size, with larger sizes in parentheses. When only 1 number is given, it applies to all sizes.

Finished Measurements

Circumference: 14 (16, 18) inches

Height: 5 (6, 7) inches (without pompoms)

Materials

- Cascade Yarns Cherub Aran (worsted weight; 55% nylon/45% acrylic; 240 yds/100g per skein): 1 skein ecru #09
- Size 7 (4.5mm) double-point (set of 5) needles or size needed to obtain gauge
- Stitch marker

Gauge

20 sts and 30 rnds = 4 inches/10cm in St st.

To save time, take time to check gauge.

Pattern Stitch

Note: *A chart is provided for those preferring to work pat st from a chart.*

Star (15-st panel)

Rnds 1 and 2: K7, p1, k7.

Rnds 3 and 4: K6, p1, k1, p1, k6.

Rnds 5 and 6: K5, [p1, k1] twice, p1, k5.

Rnds 7 and 8: [P1, k1] 7 times, p1.

Rnds 9 and 10: [K1, p1] 7 times, k1.

Rnds 11 and 12: K2, [p1, k1] 5 times, p1, k2.

Rnds 13 and 14: K3, [p1, k1] 4 times, p1, k3.

Rnds 15 and 16: Rep Rnds 11 and 12.

Rnds 17 and 18: Rep Rnds 9 and 10.

Rnds 19 and 20: Rep Rnds 7 and 8.

Rnds 21 and 22: Rep Rnds 5 and 6.

Rnds 23 and 24: Rep Rnds 3 and 4.

Rnds 25 and 26: Rep Rnds 1 and 2.

Beanie

Cast on 60 (72, 80) sts, pm for beg of rnd and join, being careful not to twist.

Rnds 1–4: Knit.

Rnds 5–8: *K2, p2; rep from * around.

Work in St st until piece measures 1½ (2, 2½) inches.

Star set-up rnd: K8 (11, 13) sts, work Rnd 1 of Star pat over next 15 sts, knit to end of rnd.

Continue working St st and Star as established through Rnd 26.

Work St st until piece measures 5 (6, 7) inches.

Slip first 30 (36, 40) sts onto first dpn, leaving rem sts on 2nd dpn.

Join tog using 3-needle bind-off (see page 29).

Finishing

Weave in ends.

Make 2 pompoms (see illustrations) approx 2 inches in diameter and sew 1 at each corner on top of beanie. ●

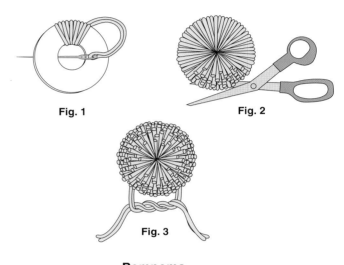

Fig. 1   Fig. 2

Fig. 3

Pompoms

STITCH KEY
☐ Knit
⊟ Purl

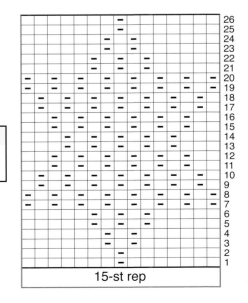

1	2	3	4	5	6	7	8	9	10	11	12	13	14	15	
							–								26
							–								25
						–		–							24
						–		–							23
					–		–		–						22
					–		–		–						21
–		–		–		–		–		–		–		–	20
–		–		–		–		–		–		–		–	19
	–		–		–		–		–		–		–		18
	–		–		–		–		–		–		–		17
		–		–		–		–		–		–			16
		–		–		–		–		–		–			15
			–		–		–		–		–				14
			–		–		–		–		–				13
		–		–		–		–		–		–			12
		–		–		–		–		–		–			11
	–		–		–		–		–		–		–		10
	–		–		–		–		–		–		–		9
–		–		–		–		–		–		–		–	8
–		–		–		–		–		–		–		–	7
					–		–		–						6
					–		–		–						5
						–		–							4
						–		–							3
							–								2
							–								1

15-st rep

STAR CHART

True Baby Blue

With its simple color changes, this baby beanie
is as easy as it is timeless.

Design by Lena Skvagerson for Annie's Signature Designs

Skill Level

 EASY

Sizes

0–3 (3–18, 18–24) months

Instructions are given for smallest size, with larger
sizes in parentheses. When only 1 number is given,
it applies to all sizes.

Finished Measurements

Circumference: 11¾ (14½, 16) inches

Height: 8 (9, 10) inches (including rolled
edge and top)

Materials

- Plymouth Yarn Dreambaby DK
  (DK weight; 50% microfiber
  acrylic/50% nylon; 183 yds/50g
  per skein): 1 skein each cornflower #0124 (A)
  and pale blue #0102 (B)
- Size 6 (4mm) 16-inch circular and double-
  point (set of 5) needles or size needed to
  obtain gauge
- Stitch markers, 1 in different color for
  beg of rnd

Gauge

22 sts and 30 rnds = 4 inches/10cm in St st.

To save time, take time to check gauge.

Pattern Notes

When casting on and working the first few rounds
of the smallest size, use double-point needles to
avoid stretching.

When working the stripes, carry yarn loosely on
wrong side of fabric.

Hat

Using double-point needles for the smallest size and
circular needle for the larger sizes, with A, cast on
64 (80, 88) sts; pm for beg of rnd and join, being
careful not to twist.

Work in St st until piece measures 2 (2¼, 2½) inches.

Size 0–3 Months Only

Change to circular needle.

All Sizes

Continue to work in St st and at the same time,
alternate rnds of A and B until piece measures
4¾ (5¾, 6¾) inches.

Shape Crown

Note: *Change to dpns when sts no longer fit comfortably on
circular needle.*

Continue to work rnds of alternating colors.

Next rnd: *K8, pm; rep from * until 8 sts rem,
k8—8 (10, 11) markers.

Rnd 1: *K2tog, knit to next marker, slip marker; rep
from * until 8 sts rem, k2tog, k6—56 (70, 77) sts.

Rnds 2–4: Knit.

Rnd 5: *K2tog, knit to next marker, sm; rep from * until 7 sts rem, k2tog, k5—48 (60, 66) sts.

Rnds 6–8: Knit.

Rnd 9: *K2tog, knit to next marker, sm; rep from * until 6 sts rem, k2tog, k4—40 (50, 55) sts.

Rnds 10–12: Knit.

Rnd 13: *K2tog, knit to next marker, sm; rep from * until 5 sts rem, k2tog, k3— 32 (40, 44) sts.

Rnds 14–16: Knit.

Rnd 17: *K2tog, knit to next marker, sm; rep from * until 4 sts rem, k2tog, k2— 24 (30, 33) sts.

Rnds 18–20: Knit.

Rnd 21: *K2tog, knit to next marker, sm; rep from * until 3 sts rem, K2tog, k1— 16 (20, 22) sts.

Rnds 22–24: Knit.

Next rnd: K2tog around—8 (10, 11) sts.

Top
Cut B and with A, work 5 rnds.

Next rnd: *K2tog; rep from * until 0 (0, 1) st(s) rem, k0 (0, 1)—4 (5, 6) sts.

Cut yarn, leaving a 6-inch tail.

Use tapestry needles to run tail through rem sts twice, pulling securely and then fastening off.

Finishing
Weave in ends. ●

Knots of Love

A playfully modern beanie that stitches up quick, this is one that will become your new standby for last-minute gifts.

Design by Trine Lise Høyseth

Skill Level

 EASY

Sizes

0–3 (3–18) months

Instructions are given for smaller size, with larger size in parentheses. When only 1 number is given, it applies to both sizes.

Finished Measurements

Circumference: 14 (16) inches

Height: 5 (6) inches

Materials

- Berroco Comfort DK (DK weight; 50% nylon/50% acrylic; 178 yds/ 50g per skein): 1 skein driftwood heather #2771
- Size 5 (3.75mm) double-point needles (set of 5) or size needed to obtain gauge
- Stitch marker
- Stitch holder

Gauge

24 sts and 32 rnds = 4 inches/10cm in St st.

To save time, take time to check gauge.

Pattern Stitch

Note: *A chart is provided for those preferring to work pat st from a chart.*

Boxes (multiple of 4 sts)

Rnds 1 and 2: *K2, p2; rep from * around.

Rnds 3 and 4: *P2, k2; rep from * around.

Rep Rnds 1–4 for pat.

Beanie

Cast on 72 (84) sts; pm for beg of rnd and join, being careful not to twist.

Knit 5 rnds.

Work Boxes pat until piece measures 1½ inches.

*Knit 2 rnds, purl 2 rnds; rep from * until piece measures 5 (6) inches.

Bind off 26 (32) sts, k10 and place on holder, bind off 26 (32) sts, k10.

Reposition 10 sts just worked onto dpns and knit every rnd until tip measures 2 inches.

Next rnd: K2tog around—5 sts.

Cut yarn, leaving a 6-inch tail.

Use tapestry needle to run tail through rem sts twice, pulling securely and then fastening off.

Place 10 sts from holder onto 3 dpns and work same as previous tip.

Finishing

Sew front and back of beanie tog across top (between tips).

Weave in ends.

Tie a knot at the bottom of each tip. ●

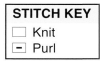

4-st rep

STITCH KEY
☐ Knit
⊟ Purl

BOXES CHART

Cute As a Button

Scalloped edges and texture work to make this beanie an intricate project. It's great for the knitter who's looking to expand her skills.

Design by Trine Lise Høyseth

Skill Level

 **EASY**

Size

3–18 (18–24) months

Instructions are given for smaller size, with larger size in parentheses. When only 1 number is given, it applies to both sizes.

Finished Measurements

Circumference: 16 (18) inches

Height: 6 (7) inches

Materials

- Berroco Comfort (worsted weight; 50% nylon/50% acrylic; 210 yds/100g per skein): 1 skein robin's egg #9714
- Size 8 (5mm) double-point (set of 5) needles or size needed to obtain gauge
- Stitch marker
- 1 (¾-inch) button

Gauge

18 sts and 34 rnds = 4 inches/10cm in garter st.

To save time, take time to check gauge.

Pattern Note

Knit yarn overs through back loop to avoid holes.

Flap

Cast on 3 sts.

Row 1: Knit.

Row 2: K1, yo, k1, yo, k1—5 sts.

Rows 3 and 5: Knit, making sure to knit into all yo's tbl.

Row 4: K1, yo, k3, yo, k1—7 sts.

Continue to knit back and forth until flap measures 2 inches. Do not cut yarn.

Beanie

Using cable cast-on (see page 29), cast on 56 (63) sts; pm for beg of rnd and join, being careful not to twist—63 (70) sts.

Rnd 1: K1,*p5, k4 (5); rep from * until 8 (9) sts rem, p5, k3 (4).

Rnd 2: Knit.

Rep Rnds 1 and 2 until work measures (4) 5 inches, ending with Rnd 1.

Dec rnd 1: K1, *k1, k2tog, k3, k2tog, k1 (2); rep from * until 8 (9) sts rem, k1, k2tog, k3, k2tog, k0 (1)—49 (56) sts.

Next rnd: K1, *p4, k3 (4); rep from * until 6 (7) sts rem, p4, k2 (3).

Dec rnd 2: K1, *k1, k2tog, k4 (5); rep from * until 6 (7) sts rem, k1, k2tog, k3 (4)—42 (49) sts.

Next rnd: K1, *p3, k3 (4); rep from * until 5 (6) sts rem, p3, k2 (3).

Dec rnd 3: K1, *k1, k2tog, k1 (1), k2tog, k0 (1); rep from * until 5 (6) sts rem, k1, k2tog, k0 (1), k2tog—28 (35) sts.

Next rnd: K1, *p2, k2 (3); rep from * until 3 (4) sts rem, p2, k1 (2).

Dec rnd 4: K1, *k2tog, k2 (3); rep from * until 3 (4) sts rem, p2, k1 (2)—22 (29) sts.

Next rnd: K1, *p3, k3 (4); rep from * until 5 (6) sts rem, p3, k2 (3).

Dec rnd 5: K1, *k1, k2tog, k0 (1); rep from * until 2 (3) sts rem, k 0 (1), k2tog—14 (21) sts.

Next rnd: K1, *p1, k1 (2); rep from * until 1 (2) st(s) rem, p0 (1), k1.

Size 18–24 Months Only

Dec rnd 6: K1, *p1, k2tog; rep from * until 2 sts rem, k2tog—14 sts.

Next rnd: K1, *p1, k1; rep from * until 1 st rem, k1.

Both Sizes

Cut yarn, leaving a 12-inch tail.

Use tapestry needle to run tail through rem sts twice, pulling securely and then fastening off.

Finishing

Fold flap to the RS and tack with button.

Weave in ends. ●

Bambini

This beanie is as delicate and sweet as the little one wearing it. Made with basic stitches, this is a project that will come together fast.

Design by Trine Lise Høyseth

Skill Level
◖■□▭ EASY

Sizes
0–3 (3–18) months

Instructions are given for smaller size, with larger size in parentheses. When only 1 number is given, it applies to both sizes.

Finished Measurements
Circumference: 14 (16) inches

Height: 7 (8) inches

Materials

- James C. Brett Baby Marble DK (DK weight; 100% acrylic; 293 yds/100g per skein): 1 skein pink/gray variegated #BM10
- Size 4 (3.5mm) double-point needles (set of 5)
- Size 6 (4mm) double-point needles (set of 5) or size needed to obtain gauge
- Stitch marker

Gauge
22 sts and 30 rnds = 4 inches/10cm in St st.

To save time, take time to check gauge.

Knit 3 rnds.

Purl 1 rnd.

Bind off kwise.

Drawstring

Cut 2 (36-inch) strands of yarn. Tie 2 strands tog at both ends. Secure 1 knotted end over a stationary object, then twist yarn until it twists back on itself. Fold in half, then knot each end to secure.

Starting at center front of beanie, thread drawstring through last row containing yo's.

Finishing

Weave in ends. ●

Beanie

Using smaller needles, cast on 68 (80) sts; divide evenly on 4 dpns. Mark beg of rnd and join, being careful not to twist.

Rnd 1: Knit.

Rnds 2–5: *K2, p2; rep from * around.

Change to larger needles.

Rnd 6: Knit around, dec 2 (3) sts evenly—66 (77) sts.

Rnd 7: *K2tog twice, [yo, k1] 3 times, yo, k2tog twice; rep from * around.

Rnd 8: Purl.

Rnds 9 and 10: Knit.

Rep [Rnds 7–10] until work measures approx 6 (7) inches.

Rep Rnds 7 and 8.

Next rnd: *K2tog twice, k3, k2tog twice; rep from * around—42 (49) sts.

Knit 1 rnd.

Purl 1 rnd.

Ruffles & Lace

So classic! This dainty beanie is a perfect pattern to get into lacework. It appears to be difficult, but this beanie will be finished in no time and will easily become a favorite.

Design by Trine Lise Høyseth

Skill Level

 EASY

Sizes

0–3 (3–18) months

Instructions are given for smaller size, with larger size in parentheses. When only 1 number is given, it applies to both sizes.

Finished Measurements

Circumference: 14 (16) inches

Height: 5 (6) inches

Materials
- Cascade Yarns Cherub Baby (sport weight; 55% nylon/45% acrylic; 229 yds/50g per skein): 1 skein baby yellow #02 **2 FINE**
- Size 3 (3.25mm) 16-inch circular and double-point (set of 5) needles or size needed to obtain gauge
- Stitch markers

Gauge

26 sts and 36 rnds = 4 inches/10cm in St st.

To save time, take time to check gauge.

Pattern Stitch

Note: *A chart is provided for those preferring to work pat st from a chart.*

Lace (multiple of 9 sts)

Rnd 1: *K2, k2tog, yo, k1, yo, skp, k2; rep from * around.

Rnd 2 and all even-numbered rnds: Knit.

Rnd 3: *K1, k2tog, yo, k3, yo, skp, k1; rep from * around.

Rnd 5: *[K2tog, yo] twice, k1, [yo, skp] twice; rep from * around.

Rnd 7: Rep Rnd 3.

Rnd 9: *K2tog, yo, k5, yo, skp; rep from * around.

Rnd 11: Knit.

Rnd 13: *K3, k2tog, yo, k4; rep from * around.

Rnd 15: *K2, k2tog, yo, k1, yo, skp, k2; rep from * around.

Rnd 17: *K4, yo, skp, k3; rep from * around.

Rep Rnds 1–18 for pat.

Beanie

Using circular needles, cast on 160 (184) sts; pm for beg of rnd and join, being careful not to twist.

Rnds 1–4: *K6, p2; rep from * around.

Rnd 5: *Skp, k2, k2tog, p2; rep from * around—120 (138) sts.

Rnd 6: *K4, p2; rep from * around.

Rnd 7: *Skp, k2tog, p2; rep from * around—80 (92) sts.

Rnds 8 and 9: *K2, p2; rep from * around.

Change to dpns.

Knit 3 rnds and *at the same time*, inc 1 st on the 3rd rnd of the smaller size and dec 2 sts on the 3rd rnd of the larger size—81 (90) sts.

Work Rnds 1–18 of Lace pat.

Continue in St st until work measures 4 (5) inches.

Shape Crown

Rnd 1: *K7, k2tog, pm; rep from * around—72 (80) sts.

Rnd 2: Knit.

Rnd 3: *Knit to 2 sts before next marker, k2tog, sm; rep from * around—63 (70) sts.

Rep [Rnds 2 and 3] 4 times—27 (30) sts

Rep [Rnd 3] twice—9 (10) sts rem.

Tip

Knit 8 rnds.

Next rnd: [K2tog] 4 (5) times, k1 (0)—5 sts.

Cut yarn, leaving an 8-inch tail.

Use tapestry needle to run tail through rem sts twice, pulling securely and then fastening off.

Finishing

Weave in ends. ●

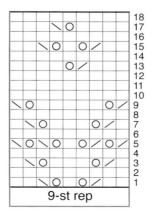

STITCH KEY

- ☐ K
- ◿ K2tog
- ◺ Skp
- ◯ Yo

9-st rep

LACE CHART

Angelique

Those who have already started using lace techniques will delight in this more extensive pattern. Knit four different lace variations to make this little masterpiece.

Design by Trine Lise Høyseth

Skill Level

 INTERMEDIATE

Sizes

0–3 (3–18) months

Instructions are given for smaller size, with larger size in parentheses. When only 1 number is given, it applies to both sizes.

Finished Measurements

Circumference: 14 (16) inches

Height: 5½ (6½) inches

Materials

- Cascade Yarns Cherub DK (DK weight; 55% nylon/45% acrylic; 180 yds/50g per skein): 1 skein raspberry #45
- Size 4 (3.5mm) double-point needles (set of 5) or size needed to obtain gauge
- Stitch marker
- 1 (¾-inch) button

Gauge

24 sts and 32 rnds = 4 inches/10cm in St st.

To save time, take time to check gauge.

Special Abbreviation

Make 1 Right (M1R): Insert tip of LH needle from back to front under strand between sts; knit into front of resulting loop.

Pattern Stitches

Note: Charts are provided for those preferring to work pat sts from a chart.

Lace A (multiple of 14 sts)

Rnd 1: *K1, yo, skp, k9, k2tog, yo; rep from * around.

Rnd 2 and all even-numbered rnds: Knit.

Rnd 3: *K2, yo, skp, k7, k2tog, yo, k1; rep from * around.

Rnd 5: *K3, yo, skp, k5, k2tog, yo, k2; rep from * around.

Rnd 7: *K4, yo, skp, k3, k2tog, yo, k3; rep from * around.

Rnd 9: *K5, yo, skp, k1, k2tog, yo, k4; rep from * around.

Lace B (multiple of 12 sts)

Rnd 1: *K1, yo, skp, k7, k2tog, yo; rep from * around.

Rnd 2 and all even-numbered rnds: Knit.

Rnd 3: *K2, yo, skp, k5, k2tog, yo, k1; rep from * around.

Rnd 5: *K3, yo, skp, k3, k2tog, yo, k2; rep from * around.

Rnd 7: *K4, yo, skp, k1, k2tog, yo, k3; rep from * around.

Lace C (multiple of 10 sts)

Rnd 1: *K1, yo, skp, k5, k2tog, yo; rep from * around.

Rnd 2 and all even-numbered rnds: Knit.

Rnd 3: *K2, yo, skp, k3, k2tog, yo, k1; rep from * around.

Rnd 5: *K3, yo, skp, k1, k2tog, yo, k2; rep from * around.

Lace D (multiple of 8 sts)

Rnd 1: *K1, yo, skp, k3, k2tog, yo; rep from * around.

Rnd 2: Knit.

Rnd 3: *K2, yo, skp, k1, k2tog, yo, k1; rep from * around.

Pattern Note

On band only, knit yarn overs through back loop to avoid holes.

Band

Cast on 3 sts.

Row 1: Knit

Row 2: K1, yo, k1, yo, k1—5 sts.

Rows 3, 5 and 7: Knit, making sure to knit all yo's tbl.

Row 4: K1, yo, k3, yo, k1—7 sts.

Row 6: K1, yo, k5, yo, k1—9 sts.

Size 0–3 Months Only

Continue to knit every row, without further shaping, until band measures 12 inches.

Bind off.

Size 3–18 Months Only

Row 8: K1, yo, k7, yo, k1—11 sts.

Continue to knit every row, without further shaping, until band measures 14 inches.

Bind off.

Beanie

Position pointed (cast-on) end of band over squared (bound-off) end, overlapping by 1 inch.

Pick up 54 (66) sts along 1 long edge of band, pm for beg of rnd and join.

Rnd 1: *K1, M1R; rep from * around—108 (132) sts.

Rnd 2: Knit.

Rnd 3: *K6, M1R; rep from * around—126 (154) sts.

Knit 1 (6) rnd(s).

Work Rnds 1–9 of Lace A pat.

Remove marker, slip previous st onto LH needle; replace marker (new beg of rnd).

Next rnd: *Sk2p, k11; rep from * around—108 (132) sts.

Work Rnds 1–7 of Lace B pat.

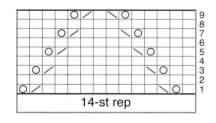

STITCH KEY
- ☐ Knit
- ⊡ Yo
- ⟍ Skp
- ⟋ K2tog

14-st rep

LACE A CHART

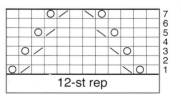

12-st rep

LACE B CHART

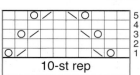

10-st rep

LACE C CHART

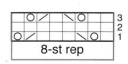

8-st rep

LACE D CHART

Remove marker, slip previous st onto LH needle; replace marker (new beg of rnd).

Next rnd: *Sk2p, k9; rep from * around—90 (110) sts.

Work Rnds 1–5 of Lace C pat.

Remove marker, slip previous st onto LH needle; replace marker (new beg of rnd).

Next rnd: *Sk2p, k7; rep from * around—72 (88) sts.

Work Rnds 1–3 of Lace D pat.

Remove marker, slip previous st onto LH needle; replace marker (new beg of rnd).

Next rnd: *Sk2p, k5; rep from * around—54 (66) sts.

Knit 1 (3) rnd(s).

Remove marker, slip previous st onto LH needle; replace marker (new beg of rnd).

Next rnd: *Sk2p, k3; rep from * around—36 (44) sts.

Knit 1 rnd.

Remove marker, slip previous st onto LH needle; replace marker (new beg of rnd).

Next rnd: *Sk2p, k1; rep from * around—18 (22) sts.

Next rnd: K2tog around—9 (11) sts.

Cut yarn, leaving an 8-inch tail.

Use tapestry needle to run tail through rem sts twice, pulling securely and then fastening off.

Finishing
Sew 1 button on the overlap of band.

Weave in ends. ●

Special Techniques

Reverse Single Crochet (reverse sc)
Chain 1 (a). Skip first stitch. Working from left to right, insert hook in next stitch from front to back (b), draw up loop on hook, yarn over, and draw through both loops on hook (c).

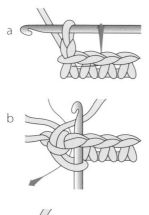

3-Needle Bind-Off
Use this technique for seaming two edges together, such as when joining a shoulder seam. Hold the edgestitches on two separate needles with right sides together.

With a third needle, knit together a stitch from the front needle with one from the back.

Repeat, knitting a stitch from the front needle with one from the back needle once more.

Slip the first stitch over the second.

Repeat knitting, a front and back pair of stitches together, then bind one off.

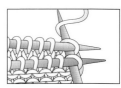
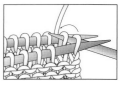
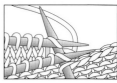

Cable Cast-On
Make a slip knot on the left needle. Knit a stitch in the loop and place it on the left needle. Insert the right needle between the last two stitches on the left needle. Knit a stitch and place it on the left needle. Repeat until you have cast on the number of stitches indicated in the pattern.

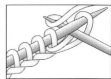

Knitting Basics

Need help? ▶ **StitchGuide.com** • ILLUSTRATED GUIDES • HOW-TO VIDEOS

Long-Tail Cast-On

Make a slip knot on the right needle.

Place the thumb and index finger of your left hand between the yarn ends with the long yarn end over your thumb, and the strand from the yarn ball over your index finger. Close your other fingers over the strands to hold them against your palm. Spread your thumb and index fingers apart and draw the yarn into a V.

Place the needle in front of the strand around your thumb and bring it underneath this strand. Carry the needle over and under the strand on your index finger.

Draw the strand through the loop on your thumb. Drop the loop from your thumb and draw up the strand to form a stitch on the knitting needle.

Repeat until you have cast on the number of stitches indicated in the pattern.

Knit (k)

With yarn in back, insert the right needle from front to back into the next stitch on the left needle.

Bring the yarn under and over the right needle, wrapping the yarn counterclockwise around the needle.

Use the right needle to pull the loop through the stitch.

Slide the stitch off the left needle.

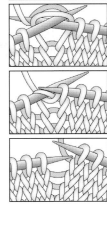
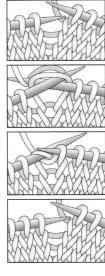

Purl (p)

With yarn in front, insert the right needle from back to front into the next stitch on the left needle.

Wrap the yarn counterclockwise around the right needle.

Use the right needle to pull the loop through the stitch and to the back.

Slide the stitch off left needle.

Bind Off

Binding Off (knit)

Knit the first two stitches on the left needle. Insert the left needle into the first stitch worked on the right needle, then lift that first stitch over the second stitch and off the right needle. Knit the next stitch and repeat.

When one stitch remains on the right needle, cut the yarn and draw the tail through the last stitch to fasten off.

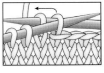

Binding Off (purl)

Purl the first two stitches on the left needle.

Insert the left needle into the first stitch worked on the right needle, then lift the first stitch over the second stitch and off the right needle. Purl the next stitch and repeat.

When one stitch remains on the right needle, cut the yarn and draw the tail through the last stitch to fasten off.

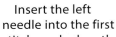

Increase (inc)

Bar Increase (knit: kfb)

Knit the next stitch but do not remove the original stitch from the left needle.

Insert the right needle behind the left needle and knit into the back of the same stitch.

Slip the original stitch off the left needle.

Bar Increase (purl: pfb)

Purl the next stitch but do not remove the original stitch from the left needle.

Insert the right needle behind the left needle and purl into the back of the same stitch.

Slip the original stitch off the left needle.

Make 1 With Left Twist (M1L)

Insert the left needle from front to back under the strand that runs between the stitch on the right needle and the stitch on the left needle.

With the right needle, knit into the back of the loop on the left needle.

To make this increase on the purl side, insert left needle in same manner and purl into the back of the loop.

Make 1 With Right Twist (M1R)

Insert the left needle from back to front under the strand that runs between the stitch on the right needle and the stitch on the left needle.

With the right needle, knit into the front of the loop on the left needle.

To make this increase on the purl side, insert left needle in same manner and purl into the front of the loop.

Make 1 With Backward Loop

Use your thumb to make a backward loop of yarn over the right needle. Slip the loop from your thumb onto the needle and pull to tighten.

Decrease (dec)

Knit 2 Together (k2tog)

Insert the right needle through the next two stitches on the left needle as if to knit. Knit these two stitches together as one.

Purl 2 Together (p2tog)

Insert the right needle through the next two stitches on the left needle as if to purl. Purl these two stitches together as one.

Slip, Slip, Knit (ssk)

Slip the next two stitches, one at a time, from the left needle to the right needle as if to knit.

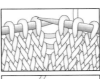

Insert the left needle through both slipped stitches in front of the right needle.

Knit these two stitches together.

Slip, Slip, Purl (ssp)

Slip the next two stitches, one at a time, from the left needle to the right needle as if to knit.

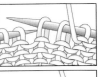

Slip these stitches back to the left needle keeping them twisted.

Purl these two stitches together through their back loops.

Standard Abbreviations

[ ] work instructions within brackets as many times as directed

( ) work instructions within parentheses in the place directed

* * repeat instructions following the asterisks as directed

* repeat instructions following the single asterisk as directed

" inch(es)

approx approximately

beg begin/begins/beginning

CC contrasting color

ch chain stitch

cm centimeter(s)

cn cable needle

dec(s) decrease/decreases/ decreasing

dpn(s) double-point needle(s)

g gram(s)

inc(s) increase/increases/ increasing

k knit

k2tog knit 2 stitches together

kfb knit in front and back

kwise knitwise

LH left hand

m meter(s)

MC main color

mm millimeter(s)

oz ounce(s)

p purl

p2tog purl 2 stitches together

pat(s) pattern(s)

pm place marker

psso pass slipped stitch over

pwise purlwise

rem remain/remains/ remaining

rep(s) repeat(s)

rev St st reverse stockinette stitch

RH right hand

rnd(s) rounds

RS right side

skp slip 1 knitwise, knit 1, pass slipped stitch over—a left-leaning decrease

sk2p slip 1 knitwise, knit 2 together, pass slipped stitch over the stitch from the knit-2-together decrease—a left-leaning double decrease

sl slip

sl 1 kwise slip 1 knitwise

sl 1 pwise slip 1 purlwise

sl st(s) slipped stitch(es)

ssk slip 2 stitches, 1 at a time, knitwise; knit these stitches together through the back loops—a left-leaning decrease

st(s) stitch(es)

St st stockinette stitch

tbl through back loop(s)

tog together

WS wrong side

wyib with yarn in back

wyif with yarn in front

yd(s) yard(s)

yfwd yarn forward

yo (yo's) yarn over(s)

Standard Yarn Weight System

Categories of yarn, gauge ranges and recommended needle sizes.

Yarn Weight Symbol & Category Names	LACE	SUPER FINE	FINE	LIGHT	MEDIUM	BULKY	SUPER BULKY	JUMBO
	0	1	2	3	4	5	6	7
Type of Yarns in Category	Lace, Fingering, 10-Count Crochet Thread	Sock, Fingering, Baby	Sport, Baby	DK, Light Worsted	Worsted, Afghan, Aran	Chunky, Craft, Rug	Super Chunky, Roving	Roving
Knit Gauge Range* in Stockinette Stitch to 4 inches	33–40 sts**	27–32 sts	23–26 sts	21–24 sts	16–20 sts	12–15 sts	7–11 sts	6 sts and fewer
Recommended Needle in Metric Size Range	1.5–2.25mm	2.25–3.25mm	3.25–3.75mm	3.75–4.5mm	4.5–5.5mm	5.5–8mm	8–12.75mm	12.75mm and larger
Recommended Needle U.S. Size Range	000 to 1	1 to 3	3 to 5	5 to 7	7 to 9	9 to 11	11 to 17	17 and larger

* GUIDELINES ONLY: The above reflect the most commonly used gauges and needle sizes for specific yarn categories.
** Lace weight yarns are often knitted on larger needles and hooks to create lacy, openwork patterns. Accordingly, a gauge range is difficult to determine. Always follow the gauge stated in your pattern.

Skill Levels

BEGINNER

Beginner projects for first-time knitters using basic stitches. Minimal shaping.

EASY

Easy projects using basic stitches, repetitive stitch patterns, simple color changes, and simple shaping and finishing.

INTERMEDIATE

Intermediate projects with a variety of stitches, mid-level shaping and finishing.

EXPERIENCED

Experienced projects using advanced techniques and stitches, detailed shaping and refined finishing.

2   5   7   9

12   14   16   18

20   22   24   26

Annie's® *A Dozen Beanies for Baby* is published by Annie's, 306 East Parr Road, Berne, IN 46711. Printed in USA. Copyright © 2015, 2018 Annie's.
All rights reserved. This publication may not be reproduced in part or in whole without written permission from the publisher.

RETAIL STORES: If you would like to carry this publication or any other Annie's publication, visit AnniesWSL.com.

Every effort has been made to ensure that the instructions in this publication are complete and accurate. We cannot, however, take responsibility for human error, typographical mistakes or variations in individual work. Please visit AnniesCustomerService.com to check for pattern updates.

ISBN: 978-1-59012-266-2

7 8 9